ACCLAIM FOR MARCUS YOUSSEF AND JAMES LONG'S

WINNERS AND LOSERS

WITHDRAWN

"Tour de force ... with crowd was leaving the theatre after the performance of *Winners and Losers*, one man kept repeating 'Formidable!' to his companion. This captures to perfection the hour and a half of verbal fireworks we had just witnessed ... The men's virtuoso wordplay is a delight ... at its heart it examines the issues of competition and, by extension, capitalism, the engines that drive modern Western civilization. The structure is centred on two friends having a lively debate while drinking a bottle of beer. But, this being Long and Youssef, some words are said that cut to the quick, and the audience is sent reeling ... *Winners and Losers* is heady stuff. Formidable, indeed."

— *GLOBE AND MAIL*

"The sly, utterly successful production – devised by Canada's Theatre Replacement and Neworld Theatre and now presented by Soho Rep – scores because of the ambiguities it cultivates. It's a game and it's not a game. It's a play but it's not a play. Jamie and Marcus are themselves, but they are acting. Sections are improvised every night, but *Winners and Losers* is fundamentally a scripted drama. All of these tensions get smoothed over because Long and Youssef speak with such ease – uptalking with conversational quirks – that it's easy to forget we're watching a show, not a spontaneous dialogue ... The play makes us question how we form judgments based on nationality, education, and other backgrounds – demonstrating how thoroughly they divide us. What starts as a sly and often funny game of differences ends up as a nuanced and unsettling show. Definitely a winner."

— *VILLAGE VOICE*

"The chatty, semi-improvised piece ... inevitably cross-fades into something more wounding, as Long and Youssef stack up their achievements, parenting skills, bank statements, and class privilege, in a sly theatrical microcosm of how people (particularly men reaching middle age) compete."

— *THE NEW YORKER*

The idea that every show will be somewhat different is a definite hook, but the unflinching and unrelenting discussion of central themes of critical self-awareness, class consciousness, and the value of competitive relationships makes this novel piece of meta-theatre a must-see.

— *NOW MAGAZINE*

"Insidiously working its way into their casual interplay is the kind of jostling for one-upmanship, for alpha male status, that spritzes the theater with the scent of testosterone … we sense roiling currents of envy beneath the friendly banter … the financial disparity between them is real, and money very much matters in the real, offstage world."

— *NEW YORK TIMES*

"Both Youssef and Long radiate tremendous charm and vivacity … *Winners and Losers* succeeds in its immediate aim, to entertain and provide satirical commentary on the cave-man quality of the winner-loser mindset. It's when the show upshifts into personal territory – Youssef and Long literally rate each other on the win-lose scale – that the play surpasses itself. Terrible truths are dragged into the scalding spotlight, something that rarely happens in polite society.The effect is devastating and strangely invigorating. One leaves the theatre feeling entertained, exhilarated, psychologically flagellated – and, perhaps, ready to examine our own lives in the uncompromising manner we've just witnessed … close to a perfect evening."

— *VICTORIA TIMES COLONIST*

"One of the most exciting, intelligent – and entertaining – shows you'll see this season … Youssef and Long keep finding fresh ways to enrich their debate: they do short, snappy rounds of categorization; they tell extended stories; they let words fall away. Despite the air of improvisation, the evening is, in many ways, beautifully structured … Throughout, there's also a teasing tension. How much of *Winners and Losers* is scripted and how much are the performers winging it? I asked Youssef about this after the show and he answered me straightforwardly, but I'm not going to tell you what he said because I want you to have the fun of teetering along that tightrope yourself."

— *GEORGIA STRAIGHT*

"One of the most innovative, interesting, and brutal theatre pieces I've ever seen. *Winners and Losers* looks a lot like open-heart surgery … the experience for the audience is exhilarating."

— *VANCOUVER COURIER*

WINNERS AND LOSERS

OTHER PLAYS BY MARCUS YOUSSEF

Adrift

The Adventures of Ali & Ali and the aXes of Evil: A Divertimento for Warlords (with Guillermo Verdecchia and Camyar Chai)

Ali & Ali: The Deportation Hearings (with Camyar Chai and Guillermo Verdecchia)

A Line in the Sand (with Guillermo Verdecchia)

Chloe's Choice

Come Back to the 7-11, Judy Blume, Judy Blume

How Has My Love Affected You?

Jabber

Leftovers (with Charles Demers)

Peter Panties (with Niall McNeil)

OTHER PLAYS BY JAMES LONG

Broiler

Clark and I Somewhere in Connecticut

Empty Orchestra (with Maiko Bae Yamamoto)

How to Disappear Completely (with Itai Erdal, Anita Rochon, and Emelia Symington Fedy)

The Last Stand (with Kendra Fanconi)

The View from Above

WeeTube (with Maiko Bae Yamamoto)

Yufo (with Maiko Bae Yamamoto)

* Published by Talonbooks

WINNERS
<u>AND</u> LOSERS

MARCUS YOUSSEF AND JAMES LONG

FOREWORD BY JENN STEPHENSON

TALONBOOKS

Talonbooks
278 East First Avenue, Vancouver, British Columbia, Canada V5T 1A6
www.talonbooks.com

First printing: 2015

Typeset in Arno
Printed and bound in Canada on 100% post-consumer recycled paper

Interior and cover design by Typesmith
Cover photographs by Simon Hayter

Talonbooks gratefully acknowledges the financial support of the Canada
Council for the Arts, the Government of Canada through the Canada Book
Fund, and the Province of British Columbia through the British Columbia
Arts Council and the Book Publishing Tax Credit.

LIBRARY AND ARCHIVES CANADA CATALOGUING IN PUBLICATION

Youssef, Marcus, author
        Winners and losers / Marcus Youssef and James Long ; foreword
by Jenn Stephenson.

A play.
Issued in print and electronic formats.
ISBN 978-0-88922-932-7 (PBK.).—ISBN 978-0-88922-933-4 (EPUB)

        I. Long, James, 1973–, author II. Title.

PS8597.O89W56 2015   C812'.54   C2014-907427-1
                                                C2014-907428-X

FOR OUR FAMILIES

CONTENTS

EMBRACING UNCERTAINTY: A USER'S GUIDE

BY JENN STEPHENSON

Here's what Ottawa theatre blogger Kevin Reid has to say about *Winners and Losers*: "And this is where it gets absolutely fascinating and deliciously uncomfortable. This piece blurs the line between the theatrical and the real like nothing I've ever seen, and while I'm sure the actors are, in fact, just acting (mostly…I think…) it nevertheless *feels* bloody real, to the point where when it's all over you feel almost garish for applauding. An experiment in realism that isn't afraid to punch traditional stage boundaries right in the dick…this play won't be everyone's cup of tea, but if it doesn't get you thinking and talking like you might be the Scarecrow in *Wizard of Oz*. Huge props to the actors, and I'd love to compare notes with people who saw it on different nights. This is theatre at its most real…and, therefore, at its scariest."[1] In his vivid response to the work, Reid captures the potent audience experience on offer, a kind of thrilled but hesitant fear that characterizes the central affective paradox of *Winners and Losers*.

After the two performers introduce themselves – "Hi. My name is Jamie and this is Marcus." "Hi. I'm Marcus" – we are initiated into the basic premise of the event; here we are just casually hanging out with these two friends as they play a witty game they have invented called Winners and Losers. As various topics are proposed for debate – microwave ovens, the Occupy movement, Stonehenge – the two perfunctorily dispense judgment. Grounded in a tough attitude of Enlightenment libertarianism, their assessment of what constitutes a winner turns primarily on whether or not the person or issue presented is autonomous, self-directed, and capable of having significant impact on his, her, or its social or environmental context. In combination with our philosophical discomfort with this thinking, our amusement is grounded in the disrespectful brevity and aggressive confidence of their conclusions, treating high and low subjects to the same brisk capitalist reduction. We laugh along at the absurdity of the game. Eventually, however, Jamie and Marcus raise the stakes and the play turns nasty when the two decide to insert themselves as the subjects to be judged. Between the two long-time friends, the knives of honesty come out and this game is suddenly a lot less fun both for us and for them.

Presented as essentially an improvised, spontaneous event, hosted by Jamie and Marcus as themselves, *Winners and Losers* situates itself solidly in the early twenty-first century zeitgeist in Canada for reality-based theatre. (Although we can trace the roots of this phenomenon to the early 1990s in Europe and the United Kingdom, it is only in the past decade or so that it has flourished in Canada.) Reality-based theatre, or Theatre of the Real as it is also known, is an umbrella term encompassing a variety of performance strategies and styles where the principal aim is to establish connections to the lived real. It is a mode of performance "characterized by: an interest in extending public understanding of contemporary individuals and society; a focus on representing and or putting living people on the stage; and an aesthetics of 'authenticity effects,' artistic strategies designed to generate (and then in some cases, destabilize) an impression of close contact with social reality and 'real' people."[2] Autobiographical performance, community documentary, verbatim theatre, theatre of fact, theatre of witness, tribunal theatre, restored village performances, and historical battle re-enactments all fall into this category.[3] *Winners and Losers* connects to this tradition initially as a work of autobiography – its subject-protagonists are "Jamie" and "Marcus" as performed by their actual-world counterparts Long and Youssef – but it also manifests an attachment to this ethos through its concerted and strategic efforts to erase the theatrical frame and present something "real." Beyond confessions of real-world personal details, Jamie and Marcus do real stuff. They roll on the floor and try to beat the crap out of each other. They drink beer. They play Ping-Pong. As we witness the crazy impossibility of scripting the movement of a Ping-Pong ball, its realness bubbles up. We feel an electric frisson at being in the presence of a really real thing. This is one way that *Winners and Losers* taps into the potent audience experience of reality-based performance.

The other way that the real is made manifest is through deliberate exposure of the usual theatrical artifice. *Winners and Losers* continually reminds us that we are in a theatre and this is indeed a play. To begin the show, Jamie presses Stop on an iPod, stopping the pre-show music. Jamie and Marcus talk to the audience. They talk to the stage manager. They explicitly acknowledge that they are in the process of creating a show: "Isn't that a rule? One of us does it, then the other?" "I thought we were just making it up." "Yeah, we are." "So let's make it up." As promised, parts of the play are indeed improvised within certain parameters. Yet, frequently, the seemingly most unpremeditated moments are those that are the most carefully placed, permanently mapped in the otherwise changing terrain of the script. As evidenced by the publication of the text in this book, this is very much a crafted work of theatrical art in the style of the Theatre of the Real genre. The script you hold is not transparently the recording of a past, improvised event. Rather, the provocatively self-imploding consequence of publication is the exposure of the mechanism of "the real," a peeling back of the curtain to "out" the various authenticity effects as just that, effects born from consciously applied techniques.

This interplay between the real and the constructed generates the conditions for the thrilled but fearful audiencing experience of Theatre of the Real in general and *Winners and Losers* in particular. In our discomfort, we apprehend the stakes differently because we have been encouraged through the accumulation of authenticity effects to connect their stinging mutual accusations to real Marcus and real Jamie. It really is quite upsetting and yet, in reflection, this is hardly the worst thing I have ever seen on stage in terms of the emotional evisceration of another (albeit fictional) human being. But more than straightforward concern for the real-world psychological well-being of our protagonists damaged by truths revealed, the audience is profoundly disoriented by doubt concerning what still remains hidden. Taking up this problem of what we cannot see, David Shields in his 2010 manifesto *Reality Hunger* identifies an innate paradoxical indeterminacy of non-fiction.[4] Fictional worlds are very stable in terms of their epistemological security, that is, in a fictional world we know everything there is to know. There are no alternative scenarios to contemplate. Anything that is omitted from the world is simply void. We cannot know what Hamlet eats for breakfast because Shakespeare doesn't tell us. This information does not exist and so we don't worry about it. In non-fiction, by contrast, the world of the historical real is fully determinate, and yet its representation in non-fiction genres like memoir or autobiographical performance is always essentially incomplete. Marcus might tell us that he lives at Napier and Templeton in Vancouver, given the reality aura created by the performance, we are inclined to take that as a true fact. But every fact we are given points to other facts we are not given. What is the exact street name and number? What does the house look like on the outside? What about the inside? And so on, spawning more and more awareness of what we don't know. "Only in nonfiction does the question of what happened and how people thought and felt remain open."[5] Thus, non-fiction is profoundly unstable, disrupting audience confidence in what we had so confidently taken to be "truth." Supplementing these proliferating holes in our knowledge of Jamie's and Marcus's world is the lack of verifiability of our knowledge. Information is delivered in an environment saturated with authenticity effects, encouraging us to accept these statements as truth and yet we have no way of checking. In fiction, it doesn't matter. If we are told it is so, then it is so. For non-fictional worlds, the existence of an external historical real lurking just outside the frame provides a solid reassurance and simultaneously is the source of serious and troubling doubt. Ulrike Garde and Meg Mumford call this destabilization of audience perception "productive uncertainty," highlighting the potential efficacy of this strategy to "invite fresh ways of engaging with people and related phenomena that are unfamiliar."[6]

What is productive uncertainty doing here in *Winners and Losers*? Fostered by the audience's epistemological disorientation, the lesson is perhaps to embrace doubt as a moral position, taking our cognitive experience of the play as its theme. Considering the play from this perspective, reframed by the experience of productive uncertainty and coloured by our shamefaced fear (we should know better but we can't help it), the question is not: Are you a winner or a loser? But rather the play begs the question. The hyperconfident black-and-white assessments of "Jamie" and "Marcus" cannot stand. Perhaps we cannot (and should not) assess the world on those terms when thinking about having an impact either through parenting (Jamie) or through public service (Marcus) or through the creation of theatre (both). These are projects combining high emotional investment with unpredictably slow outcomes. In the short term, in the space of a snap judgment, there is no way to really know if all your work made any difference at all. Winner or loser becomes impossible to declare. We might have no choice but to be scared and to live with the uncertainty.

NOTES

1. Kevin Reid, "MagNorth2013 – Winners and Losers," *The Visitorium* (blog), June 12, 2013.

2. Meg Mumford, "Rimini Protokoll's Reality Theatre and Intercultural Encounter: Towards an Ethical Art of Partial Proximity," *Contemporary Theatre Review* 23.2 (2013): 153.

3. Carol Martin, *Theatre of the Real* (New York: Palgrave Macmillan, 2012), 5.

4. David Shields, *Reality Hunger: A Manifesto* (New York: Knopf, 2010).

5. Janet Malcolm, "The Silent Woman–I, II, III," *New Yorker*, August 23, 1993, 84, quoted in Shields, ibid., section 389.

6. Ulrike Garde and Meg Mumford, "Postdramatic Reality Theatre and Productive Insecurity: Destabilising Encounters with the Unfamiliar in Theatre from Sydney and Berlin," *Postdramatic Theatre and the Political: International Perspectives on Contemporary Performance*, ed. Karen Jürs-Munby, Jerome Carroll, and Steve Giles (London: Bloomsbury, 2013), 148.

THOUGHTS ON APPROACHING THIS TEXT

BY MARCUS YOUSSEF AND JAMES LONG

In many ways *Winners and Losers* is like a regular play. It has two characters and the majority of its text is scripted. But in other ways it is not. The show is built on a real relationship, and the characters are derived from our real personalities. Twenty percent of the text is impossible to "write" because it is improvised and entirely different from performance to performance. We also regularly alter the phrasing and improvise minimally in the scripted sections. In the stage directions we have noted a few key moments in the text during which our acting choices or improvisations within scripted text can change depending on each performer's assessment of that evening's particular performance.

So a question might be – how would other people (students, practitioners, interested others) engage with this highly personal text? At the moment we see three ways people reading or studying this book might attempt to do that:

1. Treat this text like a regular script, in which two actors play Jamie and Marcus. You would then need to make a decision about whether or not to use improvisations in the scripted sections we have written. The choice might depend on the two performers you are working with and their skill at improvising. We think the script will work either way. You will also need to update or alter several subject references to ensure they stay current; for example, this version of the script includes references to ISIS and *Charlie Hebdo*, which were added for our New York performances. Earlier versions of the play referred to the Arab Spring, Iran in '79, Air Malaysia, the Euro Crisis, and so on. Approaching the text this way also probably necessitates casting an actor who looks in some way Middle Eastern to play Marcus, and a Caucasian actor to play Jamie. It may also be possible to cast two actors with a different, but substantive, racial difference and then alter the text slightly

to reflect whatever that difference might be. While race isn't an overt issue in the piece, we feel it is an essential component of the transaction that takes place between the two characters.

2. Play the game as an exercise in and of itself. We have done so in various workshop situations – from a three-hour workshop in a theatre to a post-show game in a bar. We play two basic games: (1) Name a person, place, or thing, and debate whether it's a winner or a loser. When leading the game, one of the techniques we've used is to suggest that participants think of the subjects in the following three categories: (a) benign, (b) personal, and (c) topical or controversial. (2) Pick a skill or aspect of human experience and debate who's better at it (for example, the better parent, better cook, better lover, and so on). There are many contexts in which this might be interesting to try: (a) students in theatre or acting classes; (b) groups of people who've gathered around a particular issue or question. We've found that it can be a helpful way to focus debate around a social or political issue. Please contact us through the publisher if you want more information.

3. Use this text as a guide in developing a new show that is built on the frame or structure of this one. This would involve, we imagine, employing the methodology we invented to create this show. Briefly, that is: playing the two games (above), and recording and transcribing them, choosing which to include, and ordering and editing them into a structured text that has a kind of unfolding arc or shape. People interested in doing this should contact us, and we can provide more detail.

One thing: if you decide to construct your own show out of the game, we still want you to contact us and talk to us about it. All productions require us to be credited and any productions mounted by professional artists will be subject to some kind of royalty that we will discuss.

PRODUCTION HISTORY

Winners and Losers, written and performed by Marcus Youssef and James Long, was first produced by Theatre Replacement and Neworld Theatre, in association with Crow's Theatre. It premiered at the Gateway Theatre, Studio B, in Richmond, British Columbia, November 22 to December 1, 2012, with the following cast and crew:

Marcus Youssef as Marcus
James Long as Jamie

Director	Chris Abraham
Lighting Design	Jonathan Ryder
Production Manager and Technical Director	Elia Kirby
Producer for Theatre Replacement	Ruthie Sumiko Tabata
Producer for Neworld Theatre	Kirsty Munro

Winners and Losers has been performed at the following theatres and festivals to date:

Aarhus Festival
Aarhus, Denmark

Brighton Festival
Brighton, United Kingdom

Canadian Stage, Berkeley
Street Theatre
Toronto, ON

Citadel Theatre
Edmonton, AB

Dublin Theatre Festival
Dublin, Ireland

Festival TransAmériques
Montreal, QC

Foreign Affairs Festival
Berlin, Germany

INTERsection
Terni, Italy

Intrepid Theatre
Metro Studio
Victoria, BC

LÓKAL International
Theatre Festival
Reykjavik, Iceland

Magnetic North
Theatre Festival
Ottawa, ON

Noorderzon Performing
Arts Festival
Groningen, Netherlands

On the Boards
Seattle, WA

PuSh International
Performing Arts Festival
Vancouver, BC

Soho Rep.
New York, NY

University Theatre
UBC Okanagan
Kelowna, BC

Woolly Mammoth Theater
Washington, DC

WINNERS
AND LOSERS

MARCUS
JAMIE

RUNNING TIME

Winners and Losers runs eight-five to ninety minutes with
no interval.

PRODUCTION NOTES

1.   There is no fourth wall in this piece. The actors acknowledge the
     presence of the audience.

2.   The text is constructed using the edited transcripts of real debates
     and arguments. During performance, to a limited degree, the
     actors riff on these scripted texts. In a few sections, noted in
     the stage directions, they improvise new winner-loser debates
     for the first time.

*Onstage is a rectangular table with a chair and a couple of bells
at each end. Music plays from an iPod on the table. A bag is set
to one side of the stage. MARCUS and JAMIE enter with chalk
in hand and begin to draw on the floor, creating a rectangle that
encloses the table and chairs. When the rectangle is finished,
JAMIE stops the iPod.*

JAMIE

Hi, my name is Jamie and this is Marcus.

MARCUS

That's right, I am Marcus.

JAMIE

And this is *Winners and Losers*.

*They ring the two bells simultaneously. The two sit. They begin to
play an improvised game they call Winners and Losers. One, then
the other, names a person, place, or thing, and they improvise a
debate about whether it's a winner or a loser. When one makes
a point they think is a win, he rings his bell. They begin by
improvising two fairly benign topics, drawn from recent events
or inspired by the location where they are performing. Then they
move into the following text, as edited from transcripts of previous
improvisations.*

MARCUS

Microwave ovens.

JAMIE

Microwave ovens.

MARCUS

Disgusting and dangerous. Losers.

JAMIE

Winners. And they are winners because … Jamie Oliver, the great British chef, has included microwave cooking in his most recent cookbook.

MARCUS

They're not dangerous?

JAMIE

They're not dangerous, they're safe, and they're quick ways for unhealthy British people to cook healthy food for themselves –

MARCUS

Do *you* have one?

JAMIE

I do.

MARCUS

You, the parent of small children, have a little piece of the Fukushima nuclear reactor in your kitchen?

JAMIE

Of course I do.

MARCUS

What do you use it for?

JAMIE

I heat my coffee –

MARCUS

That's why it's a loser, because we had one and the only thing we ever used it for was heating coffee.

JAMIE

What a useful tool for heating coffee. How would you heat your coffee otherwise?

MARCUS

Well, we have this little metal pot that has a handle off the side, and you pour your coffee into –

JAMIE
On your electric stove?

MARCUS
No, our gas stove. You turn it on, and two seconds later, it's hot.

JAMIE
See, this is your elitist perspective on heating coffee. Where I come from we're still working with the electric stove, and when I put it on my electric stove, it takes fifteen minutes. I put it in a microwave for one minute, it makes me warm coffee. Winner. Winner. Winner. Winner.

JAMIE rings his bell.

MARCUS
Whatever.

Beat.

JAMIE
Mexico.

MARCUS
Mmm. On food, winner.

JAMIE
And women?

MARCUS
Women too, probably.

JAMIE
Salma Hayek.

MARCUS
I love Salma Hayek. Jamie told me not too long ago, she's actually half-Lebanese, which ups it quite a bit for me.

JAMIE
But regardless of Salma Hayek's lineage, Mexico is a troubled place.

MARCUS
Well I know, yeah.

JAMIE
If you think of NAFTA, are they the big winner?

MARCUS
Oh, loser.

JAMIE
They have better beaches...

MARCUS
Much nicer beaches.

JAMIE
Better food... so they win on those two cultural counts.

MARCUS
Lifestyle.

JAMIE
Lifestyle, they don't have to do anything.

MARCUS
That's true. As we all know, the Mexicans just lie around on the beach all day. But, if we're being serious. Like, you said it: if you think about NAFTA, or the Zapatistas. And those horrible Free Trade Zones –

JAMIE
Both borders...

MARCUS
On those real-life criteria, Mexico is clearly a loser.

MARCUS rings his bell.

Which makes me want to ask. Canada. Is Canada a winner or loser? In relationship to Mexico. Canada.

JAMIE
Canada?

MARCUS

On you know, the same criteria.

JAMIE

Winner.

MARCUS

But we just criticized Mexico for losing in NAFTA, or, or, the Zapatistas.

JAMIE

Who is our Zapatista? The PL– No, I'm sorry, Marcus, not the PLO but the FLQ?

MARCUS

That's interesting. I think you just suggested that Canada's equivalent to the Zapatista revolutionaries in Mexico is the Palestine Liberation Organization.

JAMIE

No, I mixed up my acronyms – due to present company.

MARCUS

Right. I keep telling you, Jamie. I'm not a member of the PLO. I am of course a member of ISIS, but that's a very different organization. And I'm only an associate member. I don't have to go to the beheadings. The Canada-Zapatista thing, that's so fascinating. I'm going to make you think about that. I'm not being patronizing but who are the Zapatistas, and what are they fighting for?

JAMIE

I'm assuming some kind of status in southern Mexico.

MARCUS

What are they, in Mexico?

JAMIE

They're freedom fighters in Mexico.

MARCUS

They're indigenous people in Mexico.

JAMIE

They're indigenous.

MARCUS

So it's the same situation as Canada. So does that not make
Canada a loser?

JAMIE

Canada?

MARCUS

Yeah. Like in Canada, who are our Zapatistas? Our First
Nations.[1] Like, in British Columbia one or two or three treaties
in the past two, three hundred years … the unspeakable poverty,
no drinking water in some places …

JAMIE

It's true.

MARCUS

I'm trying to judge Canada by the same standard against which
we just judged Mexico.

JAMIE

But I never judged Mexico as a loser because of the Zapatistas.

MARCUS

First Nations in Canada are our Zapatistas.

JAMIE

So you are comparing a localized uprising in southern Mexico to

---

1   When touring outside of Canada, Marcus explains the various terminologies
used in Canada to define indigenous people, and those that are considered correct. He also contextualizes Canada's historic relationship with its First Nation's
peoples, usually by pointing out that Canada's policies were one of the models
for South African apartheid.

an entire nation – no sorry, multiple nations – across an entire
country. Come on.

MARCUS

I think the basic colonial dynamic is exactly the same.

JAMIE

This is Marcus wrapping his Noam Chomsky (circa 1996)
blanket around every indigenous population in the world.

MARCUS

Incarceration rates in Canada, First Nations people versus white
people, these are shocking.

JAMIE

What are they in Mexico?

MARCUS

I don't know. I'm sure they're terrible.

JAMIE

Exactly. You have no idea. Okay, what are we talking about
anyway, the Zapatista? Canada? The First Nations?

MARCUS

Okay fine. Forget the Zapatistas. Let's do Canada's First Nations.

JAMIE

Go ahead.

MARCUS

In Canada, First Nations are clearly losers.

MARCUS rings his bell.

JAMIE

Yes, but on the moral high ground: winners.

MARCUS

They win that. They get that one. It's not the best podium to,
ascend…

JAMIE

(*overtop*) There's no trophy.

MARCUS

(*continuing*) Maybe they get a medal though. Issued by the Canadian government, to commemorate their suffering. And out of respect for their Aboriginal traditions, I'm pretty sure the government would make that medal out of grass and sticks.

JAMIE

No, it would be an actual dream catcher. They'd have fifty thousand of them made in China and hand them out in Winnipeg on Canada Day.

MARCUS pretends to hand out a medal.

MARCUS

"Well done on your suffering."

JAMIE

And I hope our fine First Nations friends would nod in sad agreement. I think they would say, "You're speaking the truth, you rich, entitled, colonizer pricks," and kick us in the balls.

MARCUS

Because in that context, we're the real losers.

JAMIE

Damn straight.

JAMIE rings his bell. MARCUS attempts to ring his at the same time. Next comes the first moment of assessment. How JAMIE plays the previous "Damn straight" line and how they both ring their bells changes from show to show, based on their assessment of who is winning and how the audience is responding to the debate. JAMIE might also say "Right" or "Mmm-hmm" instead of "Damn straight." There are additional moments of variation like this throughout the play.

MARCUS and JAMIE move downstage in front of the table and address the audience.

JAMIE
I'm forty-one years old.

MARCUS
I'm forty-five.

JAMIE
Married.

MARCUS
Common law. Toyota.

JAMIE
Mazda.

MARCUS
Matrix.

JAMIE
Protégé 5. Six feet tall.

MARCUS
I'm five eleven. And a half.

JAMIE
One hundred and eighty-one pounds.

MARCUS
One hundred and eighty. Seven. Plus six.

JAMIE
I lost my virginity the summer I turned thirteen.

MARCUS
I was in my second year of university.

JAMIE
I've been told I'm the good-looking brother.

MARCUS
A theatre critic once described me as "verging on handsome."
I have a master's degree.

JAMIE

Merely a bachelor's for me. But I snapped my ankle, collarbone, broke my nose, and fractured three fingers by the age of twelve. I worked on a farm breaking horses.

MARCUS

In high school I co-sponsored my friend Kirsten's Power of the Female Orgasm club. As a kid I also got to live in a lot of amazing places: Toronto, Montreal, Vancouver, New York, and London, England.

JAMIE

Carlsbad Springs for me.

MARCUS

Which I've always thought sounds really nice.

JAMIE

It's near somewhere that's near Ottawa.

MARCUS

Right, not so nice. Two kids.

JAMIE

Us too.

MARCUS

Ours are both boys.

JAMIE

I have a girl and a boy. My daughter, Nora, is six and my son, Leo, is two and a half.

MARCUS

We had our kids quite a bit younger. Our boys are fifteen and nineteen.

JAMIE

My family lives on the east side of Vancouver.

MARCUS

We also live on the east side of Vancouver. It's that

neighbourhood, where people like us moved in the 1990s after graduating from art school or whatever. It was really cool and cheap and now it's really expensive and gentrified.[2] Our particular corner of East Vancouver is an intersection called Napier and Templeton.

JAMIE
Now a very tony intersection.

MARCUS
Upper Napier, we like to call it. As a joke.

JAMIE
We're on Eton Street.

MARCUS
Which is also very nice. These guys are close to the PNE, Vancouver's fairgrounds.

JAMIE
Actually we're at the other end. Near the rendering plant. The place where they boil animal fat, body parts, skunks –

MARCUS
It is pretty stinky.

JAMIE
It *is* stinky. But it's funny how that stink bypasses our neighbourhood and floats right up the hill towards ...

MARCUS
Upper Napier.

They return to the table, switching chairs.

JAMIE
Okay, Burt Reynolds.

---

2   When touring outside of Vancouver, Marcus contextualizes this by comparing his gentrified neighbourhood to a similar area in the city where they are performing.

MARCUS

Burt Reynolds?

JAMIE

Any era Burt Reynolds. *Deliverance* Burt Reynolds, *Boogie Nights* Burt Reynolds...

MARCUS

Any Arab Burt Reynolds?

JAMIE

No, any *era* Burt Reynolds.

MARCUS

Oh, I thought you said any "Arab" Burt Reynolds. Which I guess would be Omar Sharif.

JAMIE

Burt Reynolds.

MARCUS

No. Let's do worldly wise.

JAMIE

Worldy wise? No, let's do street smarts.

MARCUS

Street smarts?

JAMIE

Street smarts. You go first. Why don't you tell them how street smart you are?

MARCUS

Okay. I propose that – appearances perhaps to the contrary – I am in fact the, uh, more street-smart person between the two of us here at this table. My, uh, argument rests chiefly on, on what I believe to be a fundamental misinterpretation of the idea of street smarts; i.e., that it is something engaged in, uh, purely by people on rough streets. Street smarts in its purest form reflects an ability to negotiate the widest range possible of social transactions in public and in private, and on that definition I will easily prove that I am more street smart than my worthy opponent, Mr. James Long.

JAMIE

I propose that I am the more street smart because I have a far wider spectrum of legitimate street experience than my worthy opponent, Marcus Youssef. Experience tied to actual survival. Experience that comes as a result of occasionally suffering.

MARCUS

While I appreciate my opponent's, uh, point of view I think that there's a, there is a level of – I accept that, I disagree that one's survival is only tested when you're out late at night somewhere dangerous or something. I would argue that there can be a sense of threat in any number of situations.

For example, when attending the U.S. consul general's Fourth of July party as I did two years in a row – upon personal invitation from the consul general himself. It was awesome – all this bunting, and the marching band, and for lunch, both years, they served fried chicken and watermelon. It was like in a movie. A kind of racist movie, but whatever. These high-class events can also be very scary, or threatening. If you do something stupid in that situation, if you blow it, those people, they make you suffer. Believe me, I've done it. And then you're out, and you're never allowed back, and I would argue that being able to negotiate that kind of high-stakes social setting successfully requires a kind of street smarts.

Or in my political work. For two years I was co-chair of Vancouver's truly left-wing political party, the Coalition of Progressive Electors.

JAMIE dings his bell.

MARCUS

And yes, Jamie, I know that we lost all but one seat in the last election.[3]

JAMIE

A school board seat.

MARCUS

Which I would argue is very important.

JAMIE

They are changing the face of Vancouver one pencil at a time.

MARCUS

Yeah. It's a radical left party so we have more factions than elected members. But it's also serious. I believe COPE is the only party proposing policies that might really affect the situation on Vancouver's Downtown Eastside. Anyway, as co-chair of the party I was going to meetings, on one side, with the most radical Marxists in the city who make up the party's base – quite smelly guys, some of them. And on the other side, meeting and working with the green philanthropist, property-developer millionaires who actually run the City of Vancouver, and I was having open and transparent relationships with all those folks. I think that takes a kind of street smarts.

JAMIE

Yeah, and I am very happy you maintain all those transparent relationships. But street smarts are determined by where you grew up. Where you came from. What you've actually dealt with. What you're talking about right now are cocktail smarts. Marcus, you don't have any street smarts, because you've never needed them. I left home when I was sixteen.

---

3   These lines reflect the political situation in Vancouver when the show was originally performed. When performing outside of Vancouver, we just leave it as is. When returning to Vancouver, we update the lines to reflect the current political context.

MARCUS

I left home when I was fifteen.

JAMIE

Yes, but you went to boarding school. When I left home at sixteen, I moved into a basement apartment that we had to heat with the top of our electric stove. And I had to sell myself into jobs I was completely unqualified for.

MARCUS

Like what?

JAMIE

Oh God, like Michel's Baguette. *Sacrifice!* This terrible resto-café at the bottom of the Rideau Centre in Ottawa. Showing up at 5:00 a.m. to chop zucchini and be yelled at by this twenty-one-year-old who insisted on being called *chef du cuisine*. Because he'd gone to a community college for a weekend, and came back a *chef du cuisine*.

MARCUS

What else?

JAMIE

The industrial laundry where it was my job to stand at the conveyer belt and pick out the hard bits – the syringes, gas masks, lots of rosaries – from the blood and the piss- and shit-covered sheets before they went into the machine. Anyway, street smarts are not about the American consulate and cocktail bars. They're about going to the West Hotel, one of the shitty hotel bars in the Downtown Eastside – it's at Pender and Carrall – and hanging out with people there and having loose and easy conversations. Being able to work yourself into that crowd. That's street smarts. Not private-schoolboy street smarts but real street smarts.

MARCUS

I accept that, it's the bootstraps thing. That's one I live with. There is no question I grew up with upper-middle-class privilege and I've been able to make a lot of choices in my life because I am connected to that world. For example, I don't think I would be here working right now, as we are, without a pension, if I didn't think that, down the road, I'm likely to come into some money.

JAMIE

No, you wouldn't.

MARCUS

Speaking of street smarts. No offence.

JAMIE

I make my contributions. About a hundred dollars a month.

MARCUS

And I know you know that won't add up to very much when you're sixty-five.

JAMIE

Actually, it's not a big concern for me at the moment because I know that within the next five, maybe seven years, I will win the lottery and everything's going to be fantastic.

(*to audience*) Let me tell you a story about a time I was sitting in the West Hotel telling Indian jokes with these First Nations guys.

This is many years ago. We were at the West as we were many nights – we lived in the area – and we're drinking our buck-twenty-five beers, cuz that's what you do at the West. Drink buck-twenty-five beers and eat pickled eggs, and these two First Nations guys come in and sit down beside us and we start shooting the shit, getting drunk, finding out what's up – they were cousins and one of the cousins, his name was Sonny, was having a birthday and it's a really important birthday cuz Sonny has just gotten out of prison. He'd been in there for the past four or five years, he'd done something serious, can't remember exactly what, but now he's out and he's having his birthday at the

West … and we are chat chat chatting and then they tell us this white guy joke.

And we laugh, cuz it's a funny joke. Something about John Wayne–brand toilet paper not taking no shit from no … It's funny. So I go, well, do you want to hear a good First Nations joke? And they go sure. So I tell them my First Nations joke and we laugh some more. And they tell another white guy joke and I tell another First Nations joke then we're trading white guy joke, First Nations joke, back and forth, laughing away, buying each beers, getting pissed and then I go, oh fuck, I got a great fuckin' Indian joke. And I *was* saying "Indian" by that point. But we were laughing so I tell them …

These two Indian ladies are working out in the garden picking carrots, and the one Indian lady pulls out this great big carrot and she goes (*doing First Nations accent*) "Ohh, this one" – and I was doing my Indian accent – "Oh, this one. It reminds me of my husband." And the other Indian woman goes, "Wow! It's that big?" And she goes, "No, no, it's that dirty."

JAMIE waits for audience response. If one or more people make any noise whatsoever, he thanks them personally.

It's a good joke, structurally. You can put it on anybody, like (*inserts name of regional group*) people.

MARCUS

Oh yeah, it's good. (*referring to audience*) They're killing themselves out there.

JAMIE

Right. But my point is, Sonny, the guy that just got out of prison, Sonny looks at me, and he goes, "Oh, that's a funny one. That's really fuckin' funny," he says. "But you wanna know what's really funny? Watch this, *this* is funny. And he grabs my glass of beer and goes "Chhc!!" (*makes a sound effect*) Blood starts pouring out of his mouth. Bits of glass are falling out of his mouth and I'm like … he was eating my glass of beer.

MARCUS

He started eating your glass?

JAMIE

He was eating my glass of beer. And I told my mom about this years later and it turns out my dad did the exact same thing at a party one time when he was in his twenties.

MARCUS

Your dad ate a glass?

JAMIE

Yes, Marcus, my dad ate a glass. So his cousin starts going, "Sonny, Sonny, don't do your shit" –

MARCUS

Did you get the fuck out?

JAMIE

Yes, we got the fuck out. And that's street smarts. Knowing when you don't belong. (*pounds chest*) I've got that one built into my soul.

JAMIE rings the bell. He goes to his iPod.

Okay, Marcus, who sings this song?

JAMIE plays a well-known pop song on the iPod. MARCUS tries to guess who the artist is. He's not good at this game. JAMIE presses him and then invites the answer from the audience.

Next up is an improvised Winners and Losers game. MARCUS starts, usually by asking the audience for a topic suggestion. They improvise a debate about whether it's a winner or loser. Then they return to the following transcribed text.

JAMIE

Masturbator. Who's the better masturbator, Marcus? You or me? I'll go first. I am the better masturbator because ... because of a decision to masturbate less ... so when I choose to masturbate I make sure that I have endless amounts of time, I have all the proper tabs set up, I have at least five or six clips available to me so I can move between them seamlessly.

MARCUS
Wow.

JAMIE
And I commit to things of some duration so it's not just a useless flitting between this image and that because I think that's dangerous. You want to commit to your coitus. And ultimately I'm a great masturbator because I only masturbate to women who look exactly like my beautiful wife. I'll leave it at that for now.

MARCUS
Well, I think I speak on behalf of everybody here when I say that there's a lot to admire there. However, I'm a better masturbator for the following reasons ... well, sheer frequency. My second point, while I admire the multiple screens, I make a real commitment to not using technology when I masturbate. Which I think is very important in these times, when everything is going through screens. Also, variety. I find myself open to a pretty wide variety of stimuli and situations, which I can enumerate in further detail if you feel that's necessary.

JAMIE
No, that's cool. Let's start with the frequency thing. Why don't boxers box every week, Marcus? Because it's not good for you. They box every three, six, nine months in some cases. You do it any more than that and you start to lose your chi.

MARCUS
I agree with you on the frequency thing. I was just trying to make a virtue out of a vice.

JAMIE
Well, I really appreciate the no-tech thing, I'll give you that one. When I've been forced to masturbate without technology, I'm not very good at it. I just lie down on my belly and finish as quickly as possible. And it's all here. (*gestures to his own crotch*) There's nothing here or here (*indicates his own face or shoulder*)

or any pillow talk, soft touches, or kindness. It's just a frantic
attack on my member.

MARCUS

That's quite an image. What's wrong with gentleness and
taking time?

JAMIE

Doesn't do anything for me.

MARCUS

Really? Maybe it's a variety thing. Sometimes even anal
stimulation is important to me.

JAMIE

Well, if you're involving multiple orifices you might as well ring
your bell right now.

MARCUS

And dress-up sometimes.

JAMIE

What do you wear? Like a plumber's outfit?

MARCUS

You mean like Bob the Builder?

JAMIE

Yeah, but a crotchless Bob the Builder.

MARCUS

No.

JAMIE

A nun's habit. But just the headpiece.

MARCUS

No. *You're* the lapsed Catholic.

JAMIE

Oh, *I* know. The private-school boy. The headmaster's

cloak. "You've been naughty, Master Youssef! Naughty! Naughty! Naughty!"

MARCUS
Yeah, that's closer. Anyway, I'm sure no one here wants to hear the details of my dress-up fantasies.

JAMIE
We promise to forget about this as soon as you say it.

MARCUS
Sometimes I like to dress up in my wife's clothes. Just the ones that fit.
Even as a teenager I totally remember surreptitiously looking for ways to anally stimulate myself. But – I guess I've owned that now.

JAMIE
You're past shame.

MARCUS
Mmm. I feel a little bit shamed.

Beat.

Stephen Hawking.

JAMIE
Stephen Hawking? Oh man.

MARCUS
What do you say?

JAMIE
That's difficult.

MARCUS
It's a big challenge.

JAMIE
I think the only way I would want to do this is to ask Stephen himself. I'd want to bring Stephen in here. It's not a super

accessible space, so we'd have to leave him in the corner.[4] I would ask him, "Stephen. Stephen? Which would you prefer? Your legacy? Or your legs?"

MARCUS

It's a question of "legacy" versus "legs."

JAMIE

Of being able to go to the bathroom by yourself.

MARCUS

No, absolutely. What makes you a winner? You revolutionize the world's understanding of the nature of our existence, shall we say –

JAMIE

I'm not sure he's revolutionized it.

MARCUS

No? Hasn't he?

JAMIE

I think he's made it accessible, or popular.

MARCUS

Popular, okay... not that I've read the book, but –

JAMIE

(overtop) A Brief History of Time.

MARCUS

(continuing) Yeah, write A Brief History of Time. Or, go pee.

JAMIE

Or go pee...

MARCUS

When you want. And not have to ask somebody to unzip you.

---

4   If you're in a highly accessible space, cut this line.

JAMIE
Make a sandwich.

MARCUS
Go for a walk.

JAMIE
Pet a cat.

MARCUS
Do the dishes.

JAMIE
(*overtop*) Stephen Hawking is a winner.

MARCUS
He's absolutely a winner.

JAMIE
A twisted little gnarly winner. But a winner.

JAMIE rings his bell.

MARCUS
Goldman Sachs.

JAMIE
Goldman Sachs?

MARCUS
Ten billion dollars in bonuses last year.

JAMIE
Winner. They've won.

MARCUS
(*overtop*) Fuck.

JAMIE
(*continuing*) That's a bad winner. It's a shitty winner.

MARCUS grabs a pair of Ping-Pong paddles from the bag at the side of the stage. He hands one to JAMIE.

JAMIE
I'm no good at Ping-Pong.

MARCUS
I don't care.

JAMIE
Ping-Pong, like tennis, is only good when you're playing someone of equal calibre.

MARCUS
I like playing people who aren't as good.

JAMIE
Because you get to kick the shit out of them.

MARCUS
No, it's actually hard. It's challenging to play just well enough so that it feels competitive, and everybody has a good time. That's hard. I do it with my kids all the time.

JAMIE
So you like to slum it on the Ping-Pong table with us losers?

MARCUS
In this case, I don't have any choice. I'm a better Ping-Pong player than you.

JAMIE
And what you're going to do here, you're just going to keep it remotely competitive so you win by just a little bit.

MARCUS
Unless we don't play for points. We can play this game where we both just play as well as we can but at the same time we both have a shared goal of keeping the rally going as long as possible.

JAMIE
Fascinating theatre, I'm sure. Let's play to five points.

MARCUS
Cool. Rally for serve? Ping.

JAMIE
Pong.

MARCUS
Rally.

JAMIE
On.

> *They play for real. Through the following, whenever JAMIE fucks up, MARCUS is encouraging. Usually MARCUS wins (about 90 percent of the time). The remaining 10 percent is troublesome for him and pleasing for JAMIE.*

MARCUS
(*to audience*) The reason I'm so good at Ping-Pong is, when they made my dad senior vice-president at the Royal Bank of Canada, they transferred us to New York City. We had a house in the 'burbs, and my dad bought us a Ping-Pong table for the basement. He and I played Ping-Pong there every night for three years.

JAMIE
Great. Your daddy.

MARCUS
Huh?

JAMIE
Your father. Winner or loser? Go ahead.

MARCUS
Okay … my dad, my dad – well, obviously, a winner. A big winner, very successful guy.

> *They continue to play Ping-Pong. After a point or two, MARCUS continues.*

MARCUS
Although it's interesting. The mythology in my family is that my dad is a big winner. But it's in my head too – my dad's big success. I'm not saying it's not true, but it's mythology as well.

*They play some more Ping-Pong. When MARCUS starts the
next section about his dad, JAMIE grabs two bottles of beer from
the bag at the side of the stage, opens them, and hands one to
MARCUS. They drink the beer throughout the rest of the show.*

MARCUS

The thing that impresses me most about my dad is that, well,
imagine moving in 1960, from where you were born and raised –
in my dad's case, Egypt – and climbing on a plane and flying
three or five thousand miles to a brand new culture where you
speak basically none of the language and then entirely remake
your life in that place.

JAMIE

Yes, the successful immigrant story. But your dad happened to
speak mathematics very well, and he landed at the University
of California, Berkeley, which isn't too tough a place to land.

MARCUS

And thank God for the Suez War. Which meant the U.S. was
buying influence in the Middle East with foreign exchange
scholarships for Egyptian Ph.D. students.

JAMIE

Not a very good investment with your dad since he just took the
money and stayed here.

MARCUS

He's sent lots of money. And I've been back.

JAMIE

It's making a big difference.

They play some more Ping-Pong.

MARCUS

To do his Ph.D. in economics in the States, my dad had a choice
between two schools. University of California at Berkeley and
Harvard. These were his two choices. But the application fee for
foreign students was five U.S. dollars at Berkeley and it was ten

U.S. dollars at Harvard. So my dad picked Berkeley, because it was five dollars cheaper. And that's where he met my mom, and that's where they had me, and yada yada. Because of five U.S. dollars, that's why I exist.

JAMIE
(*to audience*) Marcus is worth five U.S. dollars.

MARCUS
Fortunately, it's compounded a little since then.

JAMIE
Sure has.

The Ping-Pong game ends.

MARCUS
Yeah. So, yes, uh … anyway, I could talk about my dad forever, I don't want to do that.

JAMIE
Sum it up.

MARCUS
My dad. Winner, absolutely. Fast-rising executive at the Royal Bank.

JAMIE
Winner.

MARCUS
Bought into a pension management company in the 1990s right when I bet a lot of people in this room started believing all the propaganda about mutual funds.

JAMIE
Rich winner!

MARCUS
Still if I go, my relationship with my father, winner or loser, I go winner *and* loser. As honest as I feel I can be. Because there is a

degree to which, when you have money, like my dad does, and I'm not complaining, but the money is always going to be the definer of our relationship and there is nothing you can do.

JAMIE

You mean the *promise* of money?

MARCUS

Yeah, the promise of money or the help with the house or the gift of, you know, a couple of thousand dollars. I get a pretty fat cheque on my birthday.

JAMIE

(*to audience*) Yes, he just got one!

MARCUS

Yup.

JAMIE

Yaaay!

MARCUS

Forty-five years old and still getting a cheque from Daddy. You don't have to feel sorry for me though. My therapist and I worked out how it's okay for me to accept it. But it's real for my dad. His whole life, his practice was money, he's an artist with money, very good at making it, but I think it's also fair to say that money has become the means by which he shows love. Money is also power. My dad is an immigrant. And in this culture, money is power.

JAMIE

(*to audience*) I've met his dad, he's fantastic. It's like hanging out with George Hamilton.

MARCUS

That's actually pretty accurate. Okay, your dad.

JAMIE

No. Not near as interesting as your dad. Let's do something else.

MARCUS
Isn't that a rule? One of us does it, then the other?

JAMIE
I thought we were just making this up.

MARCUS
Yeah, we are.

JAMIE
So let's make it up.

> *MARCUS has three options here: (1) ask for a new winner-loser*
> *topic from the audience; (2) suggest one of his own; or (3) move*
> *on to the topic of Stonehenge scripted below. In each case,*
> *MARCUS and JAMIE get up and switch chairs again so they're*
> *sitting at different ends of the table.*

MARCUS
Okay, uh... Stonehenge.

JAMIE
Stonehenge, that's stupid, whatever. Loser. Because it's all by
itself in a field.

MARCUS
Yeah. But Druids hang out at Stonehenge. Druids are winners.

JAMIE
Okay, what are we on, Druids or Stonehenge?

MARCUS
Let's do Druids. Come on, Jamie, those are your people – all
pink and cloaked. Okay, medieval battle guys. You know the
anachronistic society of whatever – they dress up and do fake
battles. Super fun. They're winners.

JAMIE
Show me someone with the time to go down into his basement
and make a little knight suit and a sword, and I'll show
you a loser.

MARCUS

Occupy. The Occupy movement.

JAMIE

Great. Loser.

MARCUS

No. Huge winner.

JAMIE

The Occupy movement is a loser because I know you cannot
name me five things that are still happening because of the
Occupy movement – as a direct result of the Occupy movement.

MARCUS

I love when people criticize radical social movements because
they don't change the entire economic system.

JAMIE

That was their stated goal.

MARCUS

The 99 percent, 1 percent. That language. That way of describing
how few people own how much. I think that's entirely new and
a direct result of Occupy.

JAMIE

The 99 percent. Marcus loves the 99 percent because it allows
him to lump himself in with the Mexican migrant labourers and
that is just not true. In fact, it's a bit dangerous.

MARCUS

Except I'm pretty aware I'm not a Mexican migrant labourer.
I may audition for one in film and TV every once in a while.
Isn't that the point? It creates a sense of solidarity across the
99 percent against the 1 percent that – as you know very well –
has amassed more wealth in the past thirty years than at any
other time in modern history.

JAMIE

But there is no solidarity. The Thai rice farmer isn't thinking about you. And that's why Occupy is a loser.

MARCUS

Worldly wise. Come on. You'll do fine.

JAMIE

Great. Have at it.

MARCUS

Being worldly wise, for me, means knowledge of the shape and substance of our world. And a sense of history, context, an understanding that events we get all worked up about today have been going on for decades, or centuries. And an understanding that the people we are told are our enemies might have a point of view that's worth trying to understand. Because I believe that's what allows us to act, to do things that might have some kind of impact on how our world is unfolding.

So, um, you know, for example, one of the great political conflicts of the twentieth century was the Cold War. But what were the two forces battling for control inside the Russian Revolution? That would strike me as something that is important to know, in terms of having a sense of the arc, and the shape, of the twentieth century. And who won and who didn't.

JAMIE

Inside the Russian Revolution.

MARCUS

Within the Soviet movement. That'd be one, yeah.

JAMIE

That's a trivia question, this has turned into a trivia –

MARCUS

I'm just posing questions that I think are useful. Or, for example, the political situation in the Middle East, which I don't think anyone could argue hasn't been critically important for the globe, over the past hundred, hundred and fifty years.

JAMIE

Absolutely. But I'm not sure if I should respond with other
questions on things that I've studied specifically and taken a
great interest in and –

MARCUS

Great. That would be good.

JAMIE

No, let's just do your questions. The Soviet one, like who was
fighting against who? I'd say Lenin and Stalin.

MARCUS

Uh, no.

JAMIE

After this.

MARCUS

No, it was before that.

JAMIE

Before that ... with the Bolsheviks!

MARCUS

Yeah.

JAMIE

So ... this is pre-1918,[5] like before the revolution itself?

MARCUS

After the Czar fell. What was the internal –

JAMIE

Oh, so the vacuum.

---

5   Of course the Russian Revolution dates to 1917, but Jamie has always said
1918 so we've kept that error here to show that his being wrong and Marcus not
correcting his mistake is true to the piece.

MARCUS

Who was fighting?

JAMIE

Like Trotsky and Lenin? And then Trotsky had to run off to
Mexico and disappear?

MARCUS

That's actually pretty impressive that you know about that.

JAMIE

I saw it in *Frida*.

MARCUS

But this predates that by about three decades.

JAMIE

I'm doing pretty well so far though. I got a half answer and
a movie reference. What was your next question?

MARCUS

The Bolsheviks and ...

> *MARCUS polls the audience. Someone usually answers*
> *("the Mensheviks"). If not, MARCUS provides the answer.*

JAMIE

Ah, the Mensheviks.

MARCUS

The Mensheviks were the liberals, the Bolsheviks were the
radical faction. Which I think is relevant because when we think
about the Soviet Union we think communism lost, the end of
history. But if the Mensheviks win that factional conflict, the
entire twentieth century unfolds completely differently. Think
about all the things going on in the world right now. Like ISIS.
Sure, bad dudes. But we don't talk much about how ISIS is
often supported by our NATO allies, Turkey, because they both
hate the Kurds. Or how many members of ISIS are the same

Sunnis that we supported when Iraq was fighting a proxy war against Iran[6] –

JAMIE dings his bell.

JAMIE

You got it. You're worldly wise. (*to audience*) He loves to hang his little fez on his worldly wisdom.

MARCUS

You're such a bastard.

JAMIE

Well it's true, you do! Look I am a curious man, I read the *Globe and Mail*. Granted, I go to the sports section first. I go sports, entertainment, then I float my way through the news. I'm a headlines guy. But when significant things happen, like with the *Charlie Hebdo* thing in France, I will pay attention. But if no one's shot in the next week, I'll lose track.[7]

Okay, Marcus, what if you're dropped in the middle of the wilderness, could you find your way out?

MARCUS

That's not worldly wise.

JAMIE

It's a kind of worldly wisdom.

MARCUS

I think that's more like *Survivor*.

JAMIE

That depends on how you define your world.

MARCUS

Yeah, I guess.

---

6   This topic will likely need to be updated in relationship to a complicated event that's currently big in the news.

7   This reference should also be updated to refer to a current news event.

JAMIE
And whether we inhabit the same world.

MARCUS
I think we inhabit the same world.

JAMIE
Yes. This is our world right here. And you know everything.
Although I'm very happy with my performance on that quiz.
I got a half answer. What was your next question?

MARCUS
It was about the global impact of the post-colonial history of the
Middle East.

JAMIE
Yes.

MARCUS
Good answer.

> *Pause for a second moment of assessment. How each actor
> deals with the following "check-in" depends on their individual
> perceptions of the other's aggression/passive-aggression, as well
> as who they believe to be winning in the eyes of the audience.*

MARCUS
You doing okay?

JAMIE
Sorry?

MARCUS
I'm just wondering. Are we good?

JAMIE
Of course.

MARCUS
Okay. Great.

JAMIE
You feeling anxious?

MARCUS
No.

JAMIE
You want to ask if "I'm okay" five different ways so you can feel
better about yourself?

MARCUS
No, I'm good. I just, I thought I sensed a little anger in worldly
wise. Fezzes and such. But whatever. So I asked you if you were
doing okay. And you said yes, I'm fine. And so that's great, I'm
glad. We're good.

JAMIE
Okay, that's four. Do you want get a fifth one in there?

MARCUS
No, Jamie. I'm good.

JAMIE
Good, Marcus. I'm glad you feel okay.

MARCUS
Totally. And whatever, I get it. It's not totally fair when we do
politics, or the world. But I have complete respect for the things
you know a lot about. The foodie stuff, music, culture – pop
culture. You know tons about pop culture. (*to audience*) I actually
think Jamie is about to get a Ph.D. in Tom Cruise's wives.

JAMIE
(*to audience*) I read a *Vanity Fair* article while on the toilet about
three years ago and it had one of those fun charts where they
compared his three wives. It was funny and I made the mistake
of telling Marcus about it and now he lords it over me like ... but,
more importantly, I really have to go pee. I'm going to take a pee.

*JAMIE leaves. MARCUS is alone with the audience and either
ad libs or follows the script.*

MARCUS
That's the Pee Move. It's a good one. The game is a lot less
dynamic with me up here by myself.

MARCUS gets up and gets a notebook from the bag at side of the stage; then returns to his seat.

The house next door to our house – on upper Napier Street – it's *that* house in the neighbourhood. I think most gentrifying neighbourhoods have a house like this one. It's the way the area *used* to be. The house is more or less falling over. "Total eyesore." That's what everyone else in the neighbourhood calls it. And it is. It's got actual holes in the outer walls. At one point, 90 percent of the siding had fallen off, and the guys who lived there came out with giant stacks of tar roofing shingles, and they nailed them up around the entire house. It's basically a de facto rooming house. I have this reoccurring fantasy about this house. It'll play out in my head every once in a while, randomly, when I'm doing the dishes or whatever. In the fantasy ...

(*starts to read from the notebook*) I imagine that one of the rotating series of rough guys who lives there breaks into our place. He's fucked-up on something, and desperate, looking for money. In our not-at-all eyesore-ish house, our kids' bedrooms are on the ground floor, and the kids scream out for me, which causes the guy to panic, and he grabs my eight-year-old son, Oscar. In my fantasy, I rush downstairs, in my T-shirt and boxers, and I see the guy, and he's wigging out, clutching my kid, and going, "I'm gonna hurt him, I'm gonna hurt him if you don't back the fuck off!"

At about this point in the monologue, JAMIE re-enters, moves the table out of the rectangle, places a bell at the upstage edge of the playing area, and gets down on his hands and knees. MARCUS takes the cue. It's time to wrestle. MARCUS assumes his position on top of JAMIE in classic Greco-Roman form. They wrestle. JAMIE wins and dings the bell with his foot as a coup de grâce. MARCUS is out of breath. He recovers his notebook, pulls his chair downstage, and resumes reading his story, recapping as necessary.

MARCUS
So in my fantasy, the guy's got my kid. But in the fantasy, I take

a deep breath. I look this guy right in the eye. I make contact.
"Hey," I tell him. "Don't be scared. It's all good." He's like, "I'm
gonna hurt your kid, I'm gonna hurt your kid." But I maintain
contact. My focus is unshakable. "I'm not going to do anything,"
I tell him. "I just want you to let my son go. He's just a kid. He's
eight years old. And I think he's feeling really scared."

And in my fantasy, through the haze of his panic and whatever
he's on, I imagine that this reaches him somehow, this image of
a scared child. "I don't wanna to hurt him," he says. "Of course
you don't. He's just a kid. So I think you should just let him
go. If you do, you can just take off. It's all good. I just want my
son." As the man's hand loosens and my son inches away from
him, in my fantasy, I tighten my grip on the full-size wooden
baseball bat I've been hiding behind my back the entire time,
and I aim a powerful swing that catches the fucker in the midriff
and doubles him over, leaving him completely vulnerable to
the precise blows I deliver to his back, shoulders, and hips, all
specifically designed to inflict maximum pain, without causing
irreversible injury. "Don't you move a fucking muscle," I whisper,
standing over him, listening to the sound of multiple police
sirens speeding towards us, ready to take him away.

MARCUS stops reading.

But the guys next door aren't scary at all. They're super poor,
their bodies are bent and haggard. They collect cans and bottles
for a living. When I see them outside, on the sidewalk, they
immediately look down. They can't bring themselves to speak to
me. One look at somebody like me, and they submit.

JAMIE
Because they're losers.

MARCUS
Yeah. And I'm the winner. I think it's important that those of us
who are winning take steps to mitigate the effects of that win
on the losers, as opposed to indulging in weird fantasies about
being the victim.

JAMIE
Mmm-hmm.

MARCUS
The guy at Joe's Cafe on the Drive who goes there every day
by himself.

JAMIE
The crossword guy.

MARCUS
Yeah.

JAMIE
And mumbles to himself.

MARCUS
Mumbles.

JAMIE
But he's coherent if you ask him a question.

MARCUS
(to audience) A very political fellow. Old left, hard-core
communist. Reads the New York Times. But, I've been seeing
that guy at Joe's every week for twenty years and I know he
is on the edge of no longer being able to take care of himself.
Now he underlines every single word in the New York Times.
It's behaviour I've seen before, in my mum. Early dementia stuff.
I see him, and I think, oh my God. What does it matter how
outraged you are about what's in the New York Times? You have
bigger problems than the New York Times. Your clothes are filthy,
you're semi-incoherent, and you're still reading the New York
Times. I see him, I think: loser.

JAMIE
C'mon, Marcus, he's just a little old man doing the crossword
and mumbling to himself. It makes him happy.

MARCUS
Maybe it's because I know where he's going. Soon. The nursing

home. Like my mum. Twenty-four hours a day in bed, shitting in diapers, staring at a television, unable to move. In this culture, I think any kind of weakness – poverty, disease, even just plain old aging – it's all treated like losing.

Beat.

JAMIE
Mmm-hmm. Okay, let's do my dad.

MARCUS
Okay.

JAMIE
My father. My dad had a wife for a little while, his third wife maybe... her name was Shithead. It was like whenever we would go over, and it wouldn't be very often, like a couple of times a year, we'd be sitting around the table playing *Trivial Pursuit* and eating chips, and it'd be "Hey, Shithead, we need some more beer" or "Shithead, wrong kind of chips?" And sometimes nice things like "Oh hey, you look great in that dress, Shithead" or "Hey, Shithead, I picked up the milk at the store." It didn't matter what, it was just Shithead, Shithead, Shithead. I have no idea what that woman's name was. I remember my brothers and I, we would be driving home and going "I don't think you can call your wife Shithead, in front of your children... in public" –

MARCUS
Well, or in private for that matter.

JAMIE
Right. My dad comes from a line of people who are all absolutely nuts... he's the first in his family line to not have some kind of intense therapy for anxiety or severe depression or anxiety or ...
    His mother, my grandmother, had electric-shock treatment. His brother, my uncle or half-uncle or something, still not sure what he is, had the *One Flew Over the Cuckoo's Nest* ice-bath thing.
    My dad skipped all of that, so definitely a winner there.

Good athlete, good cop. RCMP. Only high school but smart, well read. Though I remember *Mein Kampf* being on his bookshelf, which was a little unsettling.

MARCUS
Anything else?

JAMIE
Uh, other things too. There was a real fascist spin to his reading habits. Fascism and Michener. I learned all of my Indian jokes from my father. I could tell you another one?

Beat.

You want to hear a story of a winner?

My dad played football with a bunch of friends on Saturday mornings. Bunch of lawyers, doctors, big government guys.

So one day he catches a pass – he was a great receiver – and he stops, he's like, "Oh Jesus Christ, something is up" and he takes a knee, he's like "Fellas, fellas … boys, there's something up," and he's pounding his heart. Pounding, pounding, pounding. And the boys go, "Frankie, Frankie, you gotta walk that shit off."

So Frankie walks around the track a few times and he's pounding his heart cuz his legs are giving out on him, because his heart is failing or fibrillating or …

MARCUS
Palpitating.

JAMIE
Palpitating. So he takes another knee. (*still pounding heart*) Slams his heart a couple more times. "No, boys, boys! Something's up." He gets himself back to his car and sits in there for a while. Drives himself to the pub. Orders his "glass of milk," which is actually a pint of beer, still pounding away at his chest.

· Finally he drives himself to the hospital. I see him three days later and he's got tubes coming out of every orifice in his body because he has had a massive heart attack. Or a series of heart attacks according to the doctor. But he never fell down. Never fell down. Sure, he took a couple of knees but he never fell down. So in terms of that, he's a total winner.

Because he survived. Somehow he survived. Total survivor. And now he's dead. He died about a year ago. Right when we were going back out on tour with this thing. Which has made doing this really interesting to say the least.

And ... it's not ... it's out of respect to another human being that it's my mourning process ... to a human being I knew a bit better than other human beings but still just another guy.

And I tried at the funeral. Man, I stared at the picture on the plinth or whatever and tried to generate some kind of emotion for myself. My younger brother did a eulogy and he started to weep, which was beautiful. But there was nothing there for me.

I actually tried to employ acting technique to get some tears going.

Okay. (*to MARCUS*) You talk about your father giving you money or not giving you money as an indicator of his love. Well, my dad never gave me any money. He never gave me anything. And I never gave him anything back. There was no exchange and it was fine that way. That's how our family worked.

He spent the last five months of his life in hospital because he had throat cancer for a second time. They took a chunk out and it got infected and then there were painkillers and more infections and hallucinations and more drugs and more infections until death. But five months being taken care of by doctors and nurses. Of being spoon-fed. Sponge-bathed. Asked questions. It would have been a nightmare for him.

So ultimately though ... I'm totally off-track here ... I apologize. (*searches for his lines*) Okay. Some people in the world are not meant to be parents. They can make a baby but they're not supposed to raise the baby.

And if you take some of the traits I have in me that he had in him. Like how I like to be alone. A mild agoraphobia – self-diagnosed, so I don't know if it's real or not. (*to audience*) And you guys are the perfect distance away.

Or even competition. Competition, one on one, I love it. In a sports environment, I love it. But when it's a social thing or a party like who is the funniest, or who can talk the loudest, it's just, like, get me the fuck out of here.

All of these things in my father almost drove him nuts. Almost became a madness. They didn't, but they made him into a mean, mean man and he should have never been a father.

Not that we started wetting the bed when he left. My mom had a lot to deal with.

Three boys, eight, ten, and twelve. Three jobs. She did data entry for someone, some other thing, and then she did Weekender Wear parties, which are like Tupperware parties but with really shitty polyester clothes. The business model is pretty straightforward. You phone your friends and tell them to invite all their friends over because you have two bags of shit to sell them. Nobody buys anything so you bring the bags of shit home again.

We had so much seafoam- and puce-coloured polyester in our closets that if there had been a spark ... Carlsbad Springs wouldn't exist anymore.

But she turned that nightmare situation into something where she is as happy as she can be right now. Total winner. My mother is a winner. My dad though – was a loser. And in the end he totally lost. And now I get to try to negotiate this personality with my own kids. Which should be interesting. See what I learned from ol' Papa.

MARCUS
That's a helluva story. It's interesting too ... (*to audience*) As Jamie said, we've been doing this for a long time. (*to JAMIE*) But from the very beginning, even when your dad was still alive, the heart of that story, I say it hasn't changed a bit.

JAMIE
It's called acting, Marcus. Craft.

MARCUS
Yeah.

Beat.

JAMIE
Pamela Anderson.

MARCUS
Uh, okay, sure … uh … loser.

JAMIE
No, winner.

MARCUS
Why?

JAMIE
Oh, cuz she's just such a skank. And she knows exactly what she's
doing with the skank thing. Plus she's got PETA, which gives her
all the street cred in the world.

MARCUS
The ethical-animals thing ups it a bit for me but still, loser.

JAMIE
Marilyn Monroe.

MARCUS
Loser.

JAMIE
No, winner. Because she breaks my heart … because she was
such a Hollywood error. They really fucked her up down
there. But what is the image we have of Marilyn? It's like this
one. (*does the* Seven Year Itch *poster skirt shot*) Or the one in
the towel.

MARCUS
I don't see how they're winners. But it totally makes sense to me
that you would. Pamela Anderson and Marilyn, those were both
bootstraps gals. Women who pulled themselves up, made the

best out of tough circumstances. Which is almost exactly what you describe about your mom.

Beat. MARCUS makes a crass boob gesture.

MARCUS
Pamela Anderson is definitely a bootstraps gal.

JAMIE
Boobstraps.

MARCUS
Boobstraps. That's what I meant.

JAMIE
Sylvia Plath.

MARCUS
Sylvia Plath is a winner.

JAMIE
No, no. Sylvia Plath is a big loser.

MARCUS
What?

JAMIE
All the suffering.

MARCUS
Hang on.

JAMIE
Rather than finding some way to dig herself out of that terrible pit of depression, she had to kill herself.

MARCUS
What about *The Bell Jar*?

JAMIE
The Bell Jar is a beautiful, beautiful book.

MARCUS

An extraordinary book. That she was able to write because of her great suffering.

JAMIE

Okay. If we're talking *The Bell Jar*, I would say it's a winning piece of work.

MARCUS

Yes.

JAMIE

But if I were to ask Sylvia Plath, "Hey, Sylvia. What's up?" She would say, "I feel like a loser." She felt like so much of a loser, she killed herself.

(*to audience*) Marcus gets off on other people's suffering. A little bit.

MARCUS

Be that as it may, the logic that says – Pam Anderson a winner and Sylvia Plath a loser – I find that a little elusive.

JAMIE

Let me lay it out for you again. The big difference is that Pam Anderson is currently living in a beach house in Malibu and Sylvia Plath stuck her head in an oven.

MARCUS

I get that she killed herself.

JAMIE

That's the spectrum I'm working with.

They improvise the following list to varying degrees depending on the time and place.

JAMIE

Stephen Harper.

MARCUS

Loser. The European Union.

JAMIE
Winner. Mick Jagger.

MARCUS
Winner. Iceland.

JAMIE
Iceland's a winner. Barack Obama.

MARCUS
Loser. Tar sands.

JAMIE
Winner. Lululemon.

MARCUS
Loser. Pine beetle.

JAMIE
Winner. Liquid Paper.

MARCUS
Loser.

JAMIE
Björk.

MARCUS
Uh…

JAMIE
Winner.

MARCUS
Charlie Sheen.

JAMIE
Winner. Mother Teresa.

MARCUS
Loser. Twinkies.

JAMIE
Losers. Lindsay Lohan.

MARCUS
Winner. New Jersey.

JAMIE
Loser. Bruce Springsteen.

MARCUS
Winner. Outhouses.

JAMIE
Losers. Africa.

MARCUS
Loser. Um...

JAMIE
Me. Me.

MARCUS
I heard you. All right.

Beat.

*A third moment of assessment. The following two Why You
Are a Loser monologues are comprised of a comparatively
larger amount of material. The general shape and duration of
the scripted monologues remains the same from performance
to performance as JAMIE and MARCUS repeat much of the
material that is captured here. However, they also improvise new
material or draw on the larger body of text they have created over
the course of doing the show more than a hundred times.*

MARCUS
Well. You're a winner in many ways, Jamie Long. No doubt.
We've seen it all night. Smart, funny. A great storyteller.
But this is...

So, your whole bootstraps thing. School of hard knocks,
living on the edge, self-made man. There's a bit of mythologizing
in that. As far as I can tell, the joe-est job you ever had was at

Lucille's Baguette[8] in Ottawa. Not exactly the salt mines. Where were you living when you hung out with Indian guys eating beer glasses? The Downtown Eastside, for sure, but that's because you and Jay were starting a theatre company. You'd just gotten your bachelor's degrees in theatre, and started a theatre company, and the Downtown Eastside was where you could find cheap studio space. Cool, yes. But also harbingers of gentrification. Me, on the other hand. Privileged, yes, for sure, no doubt. But how much do those jeans you're wearing cost, again?

JAMIE
These jeans cost two hundred dollars.

MARCUS
I have never spent two hundred dollars on a pair of jeans in my life.

JAMIE
Well you should.

MARCUS
Probably true. But every piece of clothing I own was bought at Value Village or at a Boxing Day sale, when I've downloaded the coupon that gets me another 50 percent off the 70 percent off. And that's . . . whatever. But I think it says something. I recognize I come from privilege and I actually try to take steps to mitigate the effects of that, as best I can.

Like COPE. Who's the guy spending his free time going to meetings and fighting for social housing on the Downtown Eastside? Me, not you. Not because I have to, but because I think it's right. It's just. Because when it comes right down to it, it's a lot simpler to go off and have opinions than it is to actually try to do things. Doing things is hard and frustrating. You lose elections sometimes. And you have to talk to people, messed-up

---

8   Earlier, Jamie calls this Michel's Baguette. This mistake is deliberate and reflects an actual mistake Marcus made for a long time without realizing it.

people. Get close to them. Because that's a way that – honestly –
I feel you don't recognize the effects of where you came from.
And the way I feel right now, actually, even thinking about saying
this, that's connected to it.

    You have an anger thing. You're angry. And mean sometimes.
What really makes you mad? When other people express
vulnerability. Especially when it's other guys. Grr!

    It's true. In the mornings, if I happen to say, "Oh, I'm having
a lousy day" or "I'm feeling a little down," I see it. You're very
good, you bury it – like you bury a lot of things – but I see it in
your eyes. You want to punch me.

    Which makes sense, based on the stuff you talk about, what
you went through as a kid. But would you ever admit that? Holy
fuck, no. Or at least not unless it was here, for work. I think that's
because it's vulnerable and human, and it's a lot easier just to get
pissed off at other people and pretend that you never get hurt
than admit that where you came from maybe even fucked you
up a little. In my fancy therapy talk that you like so much it's
called transference. Jamie Long, hurt? Never! Sad? Pah! "Self-
indulgent!" "I hate when people complain! Big fucking wimps!"

    So I guess what I'm saying is … your Achilles heel, your tragic
flaw, what ultimately makes you a loser compared to me …
is that you always have to win. You have to win because to lose
might make you feel human. Might make you feel something,
anything. And as far as I can tell that's not really your thing.
Human feeling.

    As it were.

    I guess it's your turn.

JAMIE
You're done?

MARCUS
Yup.

JAMIE
Good. Okay. My turn. Wow. Very nice. You've really worked

on it since last night. So much to consider. Let's start with the anger.

It's true, anger is my default. It embarrasses me when it comes out. Or when it's called out publicly. So I thank you for this opportunity to work it out here with everyone in the audience. But it's not altogether true. It's like me just calling you sad. It's true, many mornings, most mornings, actually, the first thing I hear out of Marcus is something about how "his pillow was too flat" or "there was a draft" or "a siren woke him up at 3:00 a.m." or... It's amazing. See, the great thing about anger is that it lasts fifteen minutes and it's gone. (*to audience*) Marcus can stay sad about shit for fifteen years.

(*back to MARCUS*) And I don't want to punch you, Marcus. What you see on my face is not anger. It's utter dismissal. Complete apathy. I don't give a shit. Because neither should you. It doesn't matter.

You are such a good victim. The victim of social injustice, political injustice... meteorological injustice. But it's such a bad act because, in my humble estimation, you've never actually been the victim of anything – real. Except of your own entitlement. Of having convinced yourself that you can make a judgment about a situation like mine, that you have absolutely no understanding of and thinking that's cool? It's not.

You know so little about my history. About three stories. And I don't tell you about it because you won't have any access to it and I do not want to watch you pretend that you do. You've already placed yourself above it and that is frustrating for people who have experienced poverty and its many, many by-products. People who have actually lost things. It's true, I don't like to lose. Because when I lose, Marcus, something goes away. When *you* lose, nothing changes. You just go to another meeting.

Marcus, you're an imposter. (*to audience*) And maybe this is what makes him so sad, that he can't share a huge part of his own reality.

It's why hardly anyone in any room we are ever in together knows exactly how much money he's going to get when his dad dies or that his father is even wealthy to begin with. Unless of course they've applied for money from his private foundation or know about the place in the Cayman Islands where he's probably hiding most of it.

(*to MARCUS*) Man, you are the 1 percent. But do you tell anyone? No way. It wouldn't match your costume.

If you had stuck with your private-school network or attended more Fourth of July parties, you could talk about your money all you want. But no, you've decided to wander down into the dirt to fight the good fight with the little guys.

But imagine all that good work, all the work you put into COPE or your arts and culture policy thing actually affected *your* life. Maybe you wouldn't have fucked it up.

But you did. Because you've already won and you will always win and win and win.

And this is what makes you such a loser. Because whenever your dad dies – whether you guys are best friends or not when he does – and I hope you are because it's no fun not being friends with your dad – you get to do whatever, whenever you want. And that has made you a perpetual loser from your Ping-Pong days onwards. Shitty for you maybe, but not that shitty.

But when I turn sixty-five –

(*to audience*) When many of us turn sixty-five, and we're exhausted from working too much, we get to keep on working. We don't ever get to stop.

And even if I do find a way to slow down, chances are I'm going to be living in the same shitty little apartment worrying about how I'm going to survive the next year.

MARCUS
Except you live in a very nice apartment.

JAMIE
But it's nothing compared to your house. This thing of suffering at sixty-five or becoming irrelevant or unemployable is an actual reality for me, it's a reality for most people, and it is one of the only things in the world that truly scares me. And maybe that

fear makes me angry on occasion and I'm sorry that I scared you. So yes, I'm going to declare that my victories in life are bigger and bolder and braver than yours because I'm fucked for going after them and that is just not fair.

MARCUS
Mmm – I think a couple of people we know might take exception to the idea that you are *fucked* economically but whatever. As far as I can tell, you are dealt a set of circumstances as a human being and it's not, you have very little control over what those circumstances are. What you can control is your – how you play the hand you are dealt.

JAMIE
Yes, but *your* hand comes with a million-dollar house.

MARCUS
It was worth a lot less when we bought it.

JAMIE
(*to audience*) Yes, the market is doing him very well. It's not his fault.

MARCUS
Yes, and you know what? On the house point I concede. I'm not, I'm not going to argue with you about the house. My dad helping us buy a house was the most extraordinary act of privilege any person could receive.

JAMIE
And a twenty-thousand dollar car.

MARCUS
Just hang on a second – just hang on a second.

JAMIE
If you wanna go at this for real, let's go at this for real – divulge.

MARCUS
I do want to go at it for real, but I'd also like a chance to make my points.

JAMIE

Then make a point.

MARCUS

I'm thinking.

JAMIE

No, you're spinning.

MARCUS

No, I'm trying to put a little thought into it. Because I'm your friend. And I care about this. The debate is not whether I have more privilege than you. That's a given. But that does not negate the existence of actual events and relationships and people in the world and how we treat people. Car, yes, yes, yes. Absolutely.

(*to audience*) I mentioned my mom earlier. She had undiagnosed early-onset Alzheimer's disease – the doctors missed it. She spent seven or eight years living in a motel in California, when my kids were little (*to JAMIE*) like yours are *now*. You're right, after eight years of looking after her all by myself, when I finally got her back to Vancouver, my dad bought us a car.

JAMIE

And we should all be rewarded for such hard work with our families.

MARCUS

That's correct, I agree. But you can't tell me that receiving that gift negates what I did, you just can't fucking tell me that. Because it doesn't negate the fact that I went and did all that work. Was willing –

JAMIE

To help your mother?

MARCUS

Yes. To help my parent.

JAMIE

The woman who raised you. It's good.

MARCUS

I think we've gotta get real precise about this.

JAMIE

Please.

MARCUS

I accept your anger and your resentment for the hand I was
dealt. I accept that. I accept it.

JAMIE

Agh. The accepting thing. It drives me fucking nuts. It shapes the
whole conversation. You accept, you've done all the work, and
you're done.

I'm not resentful, Marcus. Somebody gets the privilege,
occasionally it's people who've earned it, often it's not, and
that's cool too. But my basic point does not change. And that is,
because of this wonderful hand that you've accepted, things have
been much, much easier for you.

MARCUS

Yes, but I've never spent two hundred dollars on a pair of jeans
in my life!

JAMIE

And the frugal thing. Jesus. Such a frugal man. You and your
family went to Egypt last Christmas. Three weeks in Egypt!
A family of four. And so you could do what?

MARCUS

So we could meet my family for the very first time. My uncles
and aunts, the aunt who raised my dad because their mom died
when he was eight years old. That's why we went to Egypt.

JAMIE

And then you jumped into their SUV, drove past Tahrir Square
once, Mr. Worldly Wise, then headed off to take snapshots of

the pyramids. Ride donkeys. The Middle East. The first time in your life. This place you write plays about, that you define yourself by. Trade upon. The first time in your life.

MARCUS

Are you actually questioning the legitimacy of my experience as the child of an immigrant of Egypt, a guy who came here and never went back?

JAMIE

(*nodding*) No, I wouldn't dare.

MARCUS

Good, because that would be extremely stupid.

JAMIE

I just want to know why you haven't gone before.

MARCUS

Because it was really expensive.

JAMIE

But it was Hawaii for you and the fam the Christmas before that.

MARCUS

That's not –

JAMIE

And family trips to Ontario every summer. Do you buy those tickets at a second-hand store or a Boxing Day sale? No, you wait for them to be given to you and you accept them.

But … if my two hundred dollar pants really bug you so much, wait till you get your dad's money. Then you can go and buy yourself a new suit.

MARCUS

I don't want a fucking suit. Yes, you are correct. In all likelihood I will inherit money, which I will then attempt to figure out how to deal with ethically, to put to some kind of use.

JAMIE

Can I have some? Gimme some of your money. Redistribute.

MARCUS

Right now I don't have any money to redistribute.

JAMIE

But when you get that money, I want a little bit of it.

MARCUS

Okay fine, and in exchange for the money I'm supposedly going to give you, what I want from you is *help*, figuring out how to deal with that money ethically.

JAMIE

I can chair your redistribution committee.

MARCUS

No, I don't think I want you to chair the committee. But yes, I am asking for your help. Unless you just want the money and no responsibility.

JAMIE

Please! Burden with me the responsibility of handing out your father's money. I might try to squeeze a few family trips out of it first, maybe a bungalow. But then I also promise to give it away as ethically as possible.

MARCUS

Great. You don't get a family trip or bungalow out of it though. Because it's *my* family's money. Our dads had somewhat different trajectories, remember? But I hope you'd get a decent honorarium. Do you want it or not?

JAMIE

Please.

MARCUS

Great. And you know what? I appreciate your generosity.

JAMIE
I appreciate the honorarium. But what happens today is you walk away rich, and I walk away poor.

MARCUS
You're not poor.

JAMIE
Compared to who?

MARCUS
Probably a bunch of people in this room. (*to audience*) He and his wife make – what? About a hundred thousand dollars a year.

JAMIE
Give or take. Which is about thirty thousand dollars less than you and yours if you include your daddy's gifts.

MARCUS
Jamie?

JAMIE
Mmm-hmm?

Beat.

MARCUS
Fuck you.

JAMIE
You're a tourist, Marcus. You're a tourist.

Beat.

MARCUS
Who do you look after, Jamie? Who do you take care of?

JAMIE
I take care of my children.

MARCUS
Nora and Leo.

JAMIE
Nora and Leo.

MARCUS
Really? Because as far as I can tell, it's everybody else who takes
care of Nora and Leo. If you're going to hammer me on the
money – which is real, and I accept that – then I'm going to
challenge you on real things too. You're always working.

We'll be away for three weeks touring and then the very
next night I will see you at some bad show or some dumb work
party that there's no reason to be at. Your kids are little, Jamie.
This is when they need you. But I know why you're not with
them. It's because spending time with your children, looking
after your family – that scares the shit out of you. Of course it
does. Because it means you have to be patient, you have to show
compassion, you have to just be there, over and over again.
It's called intimacy.

Beat.

As far as I can tell, your father died alone. Why is that? Why
weren't you there?

JAMIE
Once again talking about something that he has absolutely no
idea about. It's amazing.

MARCUS
Okay fine – I'll stop.

JAMIE
No, please. Keep going.

MARCUS
So what happens in my fancy therapy model is, if you keep
ignoring your own kids, they're likely to return the favour.

JAMIE
Wow.

MARCUS

You want financial security? Go back to school, get a teaching degree, become a teacher, get a fucking real job! Get your summers off and two weeks at Christmas and two weeks at spring break. Stop thinking about your vaunted art career and be kind to your own family. Or are some people not meant to be parents?

JAMIE

Is this the punching round? Are we allowed to punch?

MARCUS

You want to punch me?

JAMIE presses his beer bottle into Marcus's knee.

MARCUS

It'll have real consequences...

Beat.

JAMIE

No, I'm not going to punch you. Because you don't punch a tourist. Because tourists talk and talk and talk. They have absolutely no idea what they're saying, but they keep on talking. You don't punch them for it. No. You say, "Stay. Spend your money. Buy T-shirts." And then you wait for them to leave and you forget about them.

MARCUS

Right. Like when people who had unhappy childhoods are abusive, and basically racist, you don't blame them for it. You cut them some slack. Because you know that, that their behaviour is a consequence of where they came from and how they were treated as children. And it's not entirely their fault. I'm right here, Jamie. I don't have a million dollars in my bank account, and yeah, at some point I might. Just like someone in this audience might, or *does*, but they would never fucking admit it, because people like you would attack them!

JAMIE
Who's attacking?

MARCUS
What?

JAMIE
Who's attacking?

> *MARCUS and JAMIE stare at each other. Final moment of assessment. The following lines are interchangeable depending on who says the first "That's it." It changes every night, depending on who is feeling like they won or lost and how each actor is feeling about what has taken place between them over the course of the show. When JAMIE says it first, he tends to treat it like a question.*

MARCUS **or** JAMIE
That's it.

MARCUS **or** JAMIE
That's it?

MARCUS **or** JAMIE
We're done.

MARCUS **or** JAMIE
(*to audience*) We're done.

> *They sit quietly for a moment. Then the house lights come on slowly. They stand up and bow.*

The End

MORE TOPICS FOR IMPROVISATION

We have debated a huge number of topics over the course of the run, as shown here in no particular order. Some topics are very specific to time and place of performance; for example, garbage night in New York City at Soho Rep. Theater or Rob Ford at Canadian Stage in Toronto.

During performance, all improv topics are proposed completely without warning; neither of us tells the other what topics we plan to use until the topic is proposed during the show.

We include this list purely for reference and to inspire improvisation where it is called for in the script.

1. John McCain
2. Skype
3. Super Bowl
4. Fame
5. Musicals
6. Therapy
7. Men
8. Horn honking
9. Saudi Arabia
10. Taxation
11. The guys on *Car Talk* (NPR show)
12. Divorce
13. Infidelity
14. Polyamory
15. Middle-school years
16. Garbage night in New York City
17. Amazon
18. Mike Tyson
19. Rob Ford
20. Affirmative action
21. Police
22. Brooklyn
23. Christmas
24. Guilt
25. Vegans
26. The Senate
27. Pharmaceuticals
28. Priests
29. Monks
30. Sports talk radio
31. Hippies
32. Cell phones
33. Abbreviated words in texts
34. Torture
35. Algerian special forces
36. The Old Testament
37. Canada Post
38. Zoophiles
39. Yoko Ono
40. Fidel Castro
41. Cruises
42. All-inclusive vacations
43. Haute couture
44. *Vanity Fair*
45. The fur trade
46. The seal hunt
47. Fish farms
48. Freeways
49. Beyoncé
50. Jack Kerouac

51. Henry Miller
52. Margaret Thatcher
53. Madonna
54. Wikipedia
55. Roundabouts
56. Tea
57. Starbucks
58. Fish and chips
59. Fondue
60. The phrase "What does not kill us only makes us stronger"
61. Mount Everest
62. North Korea
63. Rob Ford
64. Talking to yourself
65. Anonymous sources
66. Marrying for money
67. Ocular implants
68. Overseas adoption
69. Home-schooling
70. White man's guilt

71. New York subways
72. Loud processing of intimate relationships in public
73. Marrying young
74. Broken Windows policing
75. NYC police union
76. Marijuana legalization
77. North Korea
78. Universal Studios executives
79. Airbnb
80. Al Jazeera

81. Beer bellies
82. Drones
83. The idea that we are post-race
84. Afghanistan
85. Day trading

86. Diplomacy
87. Hand sanitizer
88. Call centres
89. Legal abortion
90. Priests
91. Bono
92. Eastern European guest workers
93. IRA
94. National Leprechaun Museum
95. Riverdance
96. Guinness Day
97. Ogling
98. Monochrome Adidas track suits
99. Irish theatre
100. Thrift stores
101. Ethnic restaurants where food is cooked by people of a different ethnicity
102. State broadcasters
103. Houseboats
104. Legal prostitution
105. Philanthropy
106. CCTV
107. Smiling at strangers
108. Dutch fashion
109. The Wire
110. Icelandic bankers
111. Travelling with small children
112. Wearing hijab
113. Cartoonists
114. Adultery
115. Silvio Berlusconi
116. Conservative-Liberal Democrat coalition government

117. Falkland Islands
118. Quebec construction industry
119. Sledge hockey
120. Justin Trudeau
121. Prenatal testing
122. Tiger Woods
123. Muslim Brotherhood
124. China
125. Overseas surrogacy
126. Theo Van Gogh
127. Vincent Van Gogh
128. Steve Fonyo
129. Machismo
130. The Pope
131. Reggae
132. Ancient languages
133. Corporal punishment
134. Car horns
135. The CN Tower
136. Walmart
137. Nudists
138. Soul patches
139. Dream analysis
140. Cats
141. Pigeons
142. Michael Moore
143. Boy Scouts
144. Woody Allen
145. Roman Polanski
146. Silvio Berlusconi
147. Bikram
148. NFL
149. Gandhi
150. Walt Disney
151. Vancouver Canucks
152. Bertha, the world's largest tunneling machine
153. The whale hunt
154. Sheep
155. *Snowmageddon*
156. Kate Moss
157. Johnny Depp
158. Hurling
159. St. Patrick's Day
160. Irish pubs
161. Climate change
162. Religion
163. Fiddle music
164. Poutine
165. Nuclear energy
166. GMOs
167. The 1980s
168. Spell Check
169. Dublin
170. Good penmanship
171. Men
172. Optimism
173. Julian Assange
174. Uber
175. Truth and reconciliation commissions
176. Hugo Chávez
177. U.S. Christian right
178. Environmental activism
179. Clint Eastwood
180. NRA
181. Air travel
182. Politics
183. Militantism
184. Vigilantism
185. Vegetarianism
186. Tim Hortons
187. Sigmund Freud
188. Foodies

189. Human traffickers
190. Ben Johnson
191. *Waiting for Guffman*
192. Gun control
193. The Industrial Revolution
194. Germany
195. The 1960s
196. State funerals
197. Black boxes
198. Omar Khadr
199. Smoking

200. Lance Armstrong
201. Bono
202. Raymond Carver
203. E-cigarettes
204. Steve Nash
205. Your twenties
206. Talking about your feelings
207. The Roma
208. Poland
209. Iran

210. A.D.D.
211. Ritalin
212. *Dungeons & Dragons*
213. Canadian health care
214. Alberta
215. Antidepressants
216. Internet
217. IKEA
218. Lawyers
219. Somali pirates

220. Theresa Spence
221. News website commenters
222. Newspapers and print media
223. Microsoft
224. Viagra
225. Catholicism

226. Drinking daily
227. Smoking cigarettes
228. Chinese food
229. Adolescence

230. Middle age
231. Meditation
232. Golden years
233. Life insurance
234. Elementary school playgrounds
235. Communication skills
236. Pyramid schemes
237. Slow Food Movement
238. Henry Morgentaler
239. Bureaucrats

240. Individualism
241. Nigerian email scams
242. High school
243. Retirement
244. Foodies
245. International Monetary Fund
246. Mountain Equipment Co-op
247. Experimental theatre
248. Canada Revenue Agency
249. Giving change to panhandlers
250. Facebook

251. Infomercials
252. Canadian military
253. Getting good grades
254. Theatre school
255. Quebec separatists
256. Arranged marriages
257. International Criminal Court
258. Conrad Black
259. Mother Teresa
260. Family bed

ACKNOWLEDGEMENTS

Estelle Shook and the Caravan Farm Theatre; Maiko Bae Yamamoto, Adrienne Wong, Christine Quintana, and Monica Esteves; Norman Armour and the PuSh Festival; Simon Johnston, Kathy Duborg, and the Gateway Theatre; Canada Council for the Arts, B.C. Arts Council, and the City of Vancouver; and everyone at Talonbooks.

MARCUS YOUSSEF

The ethic and practice of collaboration are central to Marcus Youssef's creative work. His plays and performance events have been performed in every major Canadian city, across North America and Australia, and as part of major European festivals. Youssef has received multiple awards, including Rio-Tinto Alcan Performing Arts, Chalmer's Canadian Play, Arts Club Silver Commission, Seattle Times Footlight, Vancouver Critics' Choice Innovation (three times), as well as numerous local Canadian awards and nominations for best new play, production, performance, and director. He has been artistic director of Vancouver's Neworld Theatre since 2005, where he also co-founded PL1422, a collaboratively managed, six-thousand-square-foot studio and production hub. Youssef teaches regularly at the National Theatre School of Canada and Langara College's Studio 58, and sits on the advisory board of *Canadian Theatre Review*. His journalism and fiction are also published and broadcast widely. He lives in East Vancouver with his partner, teacher Amanda Fritzlan, and their sons Oscar and Zak.

JAMES LONG

James Long has been making theatre since 1995 and founded Theatre Replacement with Maiko Bae Yamamoto in 2003. The company's work has been presented in thirty-nine cities and venues across North America and Europe and includes *Clark and I Somewhere in Connecticut, BIOBOXES: Artifacting Human Experience, Sexual Practices of the Japanese, Weetube, Dress me up in your love, The Greatest Cities in the World, Winners and Losers,* and *Kate Bowie,* among others. Long has worked as a freelance writer and actor with Rumble Productions, Neworld, urban ink, The Only Animal, CBC Radio, and The Electric Company, among many others. Freelance directorial work includes *Morko,* a site-oriented performance created with visual artist and animator Cindy Mochizuki and *How to Disappear Completely,* created for the Chop Theatre with lighting designer Itai Erdal. Long has also taught performance and methods of creation to established artists across Canada and to students at the University of British Columbia, University of Regina, Simon Fraser University, Langara College's Studio 58, and Seattle's Cornish College of the Arts. He is a graduate of SFU's School of Contemporary Arts.